THE CHEQUERED SHADE

THE CHEQUERED

POEMS BY ROY DANIELLS

Contents

 *for* aurenda

WHERE THE GREAT CAESAR CAME

Menton 1

Here come I where the great Caesar came,
In these small Alps his smaller trophy left,
As the older Greek (black prow in Monaco bay)
Left a black jar in the white rock's cleft.
They say there was sunburned mirth in old Provence,
Then Bourbons or Directory on the march,
Napoleons, Monte Carlo, last La France,
Leaving death, destruction, faith and the fine arts.
And what shall I leave? Only this tentative song
Of love for the azure coast, the luminous wave,
The palm, the divulging orange, the rusty vine,
The moving eye of this boy who rambles along,
This white stone reared to Resistance, names of the brave.
Remembering them, what heart shall not incline?

Menton 2

Cypresses and the worn sandstone hide
My foolish tears, while the refulgent dome
Divulges warmth on tombs. Here far from home
The Sussex girl who reached Menton and died,
Or the young officer, the invalid
From India. Never to see the white cliffs come
Down to the Channel waves, their whiter foam.
They, whom no care or love could save, indeed
Are cause for tears delayed. But not for these
Nor for the wandering grief of the wide earth
My tears flow now. But for grief undefined
That neither tears nor comforts can appease.
Far as imagined space its place of birth,
Sharp as your mind's abyss, torn as the wind.

Menton 3

They say that often this small plain under the sand-
Stone terraces climbing the hills beside the sea,
With its thin streams and its weaving olive tree,
And huddled houses on a crowded strand,
Saw armies pass to where the late sun burned
On Italy. Or in recoiling march
Dragged their maimed way through this one narrow arch
And with their wounded to this spot returned
And found compassion.
                    They poured in oil and wine,
Though harried ever by armies age by age.
Under the silver leaves the wounded lay,
By the olive, the willow and the leaning vine.
Compassion met them with her power to assuage,
And this sure sun revived their languid day.

Ste Agnes

uin, decay, and smell of the peeled plaster.
The stones, once fitted, fallen or fit to fall.
A boy mending his bicycle by the wall
Ready to mount, to leap fast and faster
Down the swift slope to look for a new master.
Two camions toil to the fort, highest of all,
Whence Hitler's shots fired, fired our ships, small
In the blue bay below, a last disaster.
                                    Yet in the rock
The saint stands ready to bless; the flowers unwithered
Freshly and freshly placed by the few hands
Smile. Time suddenly stops, and with the shock
The fort flies off. By slender centuries tethered,
The smiling girl with her phantom village stands.

Peille

ere stones climb, helped by hands, up glacis of mountains,
Terrace lends a shoulder to terrace; tiles by tiles
Small roofs have inched their height toward the ridges.
On their tensed haunches little eager bridges
Leap over gorges. The sullen limestone piles
High into sunlight, holding its leash of fountains.

I who every morning took out a team
In flat Saskatchewan and found the disks
A point in space stretching without shade
Have laid straight furrows until late sun made
Faint shadows race from our abandoned tasks
While home we strayed in his delaying flames.

Col de Tende

It seemed the mind might leave its thoughts behind
Lost in La Roya leaping down its ridges,
Lost in spray from the falls, rain in the wind,
While the road curled under the rock and the wrecked bridges.
All the way up white villages back to the wall
High as they could climb, and Tende beckoned
The mind, like a refuge, forward; highest of all
Up on its col. It was not quite what I'd reckoned.
But repose on an edge. The waters hurried away;
A tunnel pulled toward Turin, to Nice a cleft,
Like an equals sign where unstable equations sway.
(High level bridges all blown when the Germans left.)
We shan't be here again. But do not grieve;
This is the place I think we shall not leave.

Florence

This is no place for burning; only the flowers
Offer their cool flames to the gentle air,
And one who lit the fire that in this square
Consumed the vanities, by violent powers
Was here consumed. And still the cool stone towers
In Botticelli's sky. One, stair by stair,
Descending into hell's revealing flare,
They could not bear, and all succeeding hours
His flames must burn elsewhere.
                                        Who may regret it?
Here, if here only, gentleness must ascend
Into the ascendant with Angelico.
The passion and all the pain, who may forget it?
(And they their recompense receive at end.)
But here let peace with pensive Arno flow.

Storm over Livorno

Shelley, staring at torn skies in delight
Saw rain and lightning burst where upward flowed
The Maenad's streaming hair, a rising road
For galloping winds up to the zenith's height.
Skies were enormous halls of Day and Night
Of Powers of Earth and Air, from whose abode
The lights of everlasting freedom glowed
Above our fogs, in their unfailing Light.

Leaning toward the skies, he drowned out there.
They burned him on this beach, threw oil and wine
Into the flames. O well for his desires!
Our skies, with fear congested everywhere,
Our skies, with menace for their countersign,
Give warning of his hopes, fire on his fires.

With Children in the Protestant Cemetery

Kneel in the grass with them. And when you say,
"He was a poet, you will love him, he died young,
See here his face and the words from Shelley's tongue
Set in enduring marble, look! this way,"
Go on, go on, to tell what day by day
Through years nor Keats nor Shelley could prolong
You've learned, that bitterness and grief and wrong
Time hurls upon us, friendship lifts away.
Point to the stone set here for gentle Severn,
Honour rewarding that all-faithful friend;
Then take their hands, lead through the April flowers
To where beneath the cypress-dappled cavern
Of shadow bold Trelawny willed his end
By Shelley. Show them love and friendship's powers.

Sonnet for George and William

I stood in Venice on the Bridge of Sighs,
On either hand a palace and a prison.
Miraculous from sea her splendours rise,
But many must have wished they'd never risen.
Another hour of old blind Dandolo
Is more than heaven or Istanbul could bear;
Wild horses, leaping toward the land they know,
Would tear his limbs upon the trackless air.
Napoleon burned Bucentaur, and who grieves
At end of secret trials, assassinations,
And all the sad variety that thieves
Inflict upon their own and other nations?
Extinction suits old Venice very well;
New winds, new waters, sweep the Grand Canal.

Golden Horn

arry the pine and terebinth, then lay
His dark bones on the pyre, dredged from the tide
By love and care that searching night and day
Drew them up on this European side.
Then put the fire beneath them, sprinkle salt,
Cast in the wine, the oil; let fall your tears;
And watch the bright flame climbing heaven's vault
Perpetuate his passion through the years.
No act of worship his, no social rite,
No prudent labour, calculated gain.
He leaped into this Hellespont by night
For sight of Hero and to ease the pain
Of love, and these alone were his endeavour.
And these suffice Leander's fame forever.

Low Countries

Easy to reckon them invulnerable
These fishermen and farmers lapped in toil,
Able to tame with force unconquerable
Even their guardians, the deep sea and soil.
Timber, wattle and clay their cottages,
Tiled over or thatched in. There on the wall
Luther's uplifted hand admonishes
The prince. At hand are cattle in the stall.
Floods from the bitter sky and sea unharnessed
Have over house and dike and polder rolled.
Fire fell from heaven. Fierce and furious armies
Hacked at them, blasted, broke their hold.
And may again. Yet their great story strides
In all our hearts and minds, through winds and tides.

London 1

Not column, statue, famous tower or steeple
In London's streets I see, but Gargery, Squeers,
Fagin and Sykes, and all his ceaseless people,
Over the road Micawber's head appears.
The beach was crowded and the air was warm
On Yarmouth sands, the merriment rang loud;
But on an outstretched arm, after the storm,
One face was all I saw, beyond the crowd.
Within those walls of Paris, sombre, high,
That fierce despair and courage once possessed
Doomed to the falling blade, what met my eye
Was only Carton, moving toward his rest,
And on Italian shores in sunlight drowned
One wandering girl whom her fond uncle found.

London 2

A pair of straightened scythe-blades nailed to poles
Hung in the Tower of London on the wall;
As weapons hardly any use at all.
The chaps who held them, they were simple souls.
Artillery up on the hill ripped holes
In their unsteady line, volleys of ball
Across the ditch made these poor fellows fall,
Ignoble fall that never church bell tolls,
At Sedgemoor long ago.
                           Then Jeffreys came
And hanged them by the hundreds at their doors
And exiled thousands into bonds of shame
And left a sound of weeping on the moors.
But I will touch these blades, their still dark flame,
And say, "Your cause was mine and mine is yours."

London 3

The house where I was born, recalled by Love
From long concealment in the indifferent past,
Bricks and beams blown by a bomb's blast
To oblivion, leaving only the pattern above
That Plato told. This I with care recover,
Find in the mind's fold the form recast,
Not cold, nor hot in time's impetuous haste.
Quiet in the mind of form's eternal lover,
Who shapes and who sustains.
                                        The guardian powers
Are here upheld, of door, of hearth, of wall,
The well-loved leaves and blossoms keep their kind
Unhastened by old harsh persistent hours.
And when this mind to formlessness shall fall
My thoughts their form in that same love shall find.

Zoological Gardens

They do not do so badly, all and one,
Down the wild wishful aeons they persist,
Not all arriving, but defaulters missed
Not on parade, have sent their badges on
Whose cryptic Latin beats the lexicon.
But who – and pardon me if I insist –
After all changes by the alchemist,
Who, when your tribe makes ready to be gone,
Will want to keep your kind?
                                    I ask you, who
For love, for intellectual dividend,
Will raise the cash and build a little zoo
For you? Who cares if you come to an end?
Who as a specimen would write on you?
Who wants to keep your kin or kind, my friend?

Re-Creation Grounds

See where the simple swan with arched neck
Between her white wings mantling proudly rows
Her state with oary feet. The schoolboy knows
That Milton saw her thus complete. The Rec
At Palmer's Green sees her, an alimbec
Distilling beauty's essence; softly flows
The smooth stream; here she preens; her presence grows
One with dark waters flowing without check.

There will be swans long after we are gone,
Heraldic double-headers, in mutations,
Their galleys many-oared, till the great strain
Shall reassert itself; though men move on
To end of mankind or the end of nations,
Streams shall reflect her simple state again.

Broomfield Park

Once it was moored in the long undulant swell
Where hedgerows leaning hardly could contain
The green tides. Here the billowing summer fell,
Then the slow ebb of autumn, in sighing rain.
Stiff with its timbered pargeting, and square
With serried elms and vista to the gate
And small set silver lakes with one white pair,
It held the inebriate country off, sedate.

Now amid maze of brick and slate and tile,
Of ceaseless concrete, asphalt, wires and towers,
With red and green eyes staring mile on mile,
This pool of verdure, wavering walls and flowers,
Float like a dream in some old brain that keeps
A loved, slow-swimming image while it sleeps.

Fire on the Rock. Its spires ascending quiver
And rend night's sky. See the incendiary stones
Reverberate the white fires of the nuns
While far beneath the deep enkindled River
Renders its foam and fiery flakes of fever
To the dark Gulf. The virtuous skull here crowns
All valiant bones, by its own lambence shines.
From plains above, loud and distinct forever,
The firing rolls.

           O city militant,
With martial fire your sign and attribute,
With martyrs' folded flame strongly possessed,
Still from your Cape I hear the mighty chant
Where Iroquois burned, burned retributive.
I think of fires in clearings far to West.

Quebec

Mosaic

Child of concealment in the heart of Water,
Ripples and reeds flow all about his ark;
He melts with loneliness till Pharaoh's daughter
Divines his tears and draws him from the dark.
The waste of wilderness, the flocks in keeping,
The sun that strikes: no mind can here aspire.
Yet see where suddenly the red flame leaping
Bursts from a bush and voices fill the Fire.
Far in the upper Air, the mount of vision,
He hears the doom of law, the gift of grace,
And from that firmament of high decision
Descends with light transfiguring his face.
And at the close when he resigns his care
The Earth lies open, angels lay him there.

Noah 1

obody feels for Noah the least affection,
And yet he laboured hard from dawn to dark
With hammer and plane and tar-brush on the ark
And brought his sons to work at his direction.
The unclean animals, for their own protection,
Came two by two to his enormous barque
And seven by seven (the facts are somewhat stark)
The clean ones to his commissariat section
Five to be slaughtered.
     Next the poor old fellow,
The long voyage over, paid off all the crew,
Lay down upon dry ground and took a drink,
Then cursed the black son, blessed the white and yellow
(Who only did what you or I might do).
A patriarch, – but not much loved I think.

Noah 2

They gathered around and told him not to do it,
They formed a committee and tried to take control,
They cancelled his building permit and they stole
His plans. I sometimes wonder he got through it.
He told them wrath was coming, they would rue it,
He begged them to believe the tides would roll,
He offered them passage to his destined goal,
A new world. They were finished and he knew it.
All to no end.
                    And then the rain began.
A spatter at first that barely wet the soil,
Then showers, quick rivulets lacing the town,
Then deluge universal. The old man
Arthritic from his years of scorn and toil
Leaned from the admiral's walk and watched them drown.

Leviticus 16:22

They hauled the halter off his hairy neck
And walked away. I wonder what he did.
If he settled down to make the long hard trek
To the other side of the Sea. If he merely hid.
Whatever course he adopted, there's no doubt
He was heavily burdened with a sense of guilt.
The whole community rose and thrust him out;
He was thick with sin as a river mouth with silt.
Perhaps by watching his step he kept his balance;
And met with others, others of his own kind,
Descended to mix with them, not hide his talents,
Played with the kids, let the past fall behind.
Freud, Adler, Jung, they all unite to tell
A scapegoat's life must simply have been hell.

Numbers 22:26-31

The one clear indisputable voice
Is that of the ass. I think she had a case.
Balaam struck her twice, in the narrow place
Where the angel stood in the path. She had no choice.
She was frightened, she lost her equipoise,
She fell to the earth in terror and disgrace.
But not her fault; there wasn't an inch of space.
The invisible angel without stir or noise
Straddled the way.
     Balaam in Israel's slaughter
Of enemies was slain, the books declare,
With men and captive women and boys. The sun
Shone upon blood that flowed like Jordan's water.
Three score asses and one were Jehovah's share.
I like to think that she was that last one.

Psalm 23

y enemies were certain I was starving,
It must have given them a fearful shock
Through the binoculars to see me carving
A roast of beef up on the barren rock.
And when I moved upon them down a byway,
Bathed and anointed, sweet with oil of rose,
They blanched for they had left me on the highway
Covered with blood and with a broken nose.
The landlord, in the arbour where I'm seated,
Has brimmed the bowl with wine, the bubbles wink.
It's time my gasping enemies were treated,
Do tell them to come in and have a drink.
And any day they like they may appear;
Thanks to the landlord, I'll be living here.

Psalm 37

Fret not thyself because of evil-doers.
Good advice but very hard to take.
Too many bastards always on the make;
Too many heiresses with crafty wooers;
Too many who for beer would kill the brewers;
Too many justice fails to overtake;
Too many hands that want my bit of cake;
Too many lords with seneschals and sewers.

The Lord shall laugh at them I do not doubt,
The Lord shall hold them in a high derision
And break their bloody eye-teeth on the stones.
But in the meantime how to go about
Containing myself. For that there's no provision.
Anger and hope deferred eat out my bones.

Psalm 57

Forgive me Lord, but not my enemies.
Or else install another mind in mine
A switchboard of superior design
Shortcircuiting my dearest enmities
So that the current of my miseries
Charging the sullen earth, shall then resign
To wait until that gathering wrath of thine
Fills all the sky with dark immensities
Of storm impending. Then at deep midnight
While they are met to plot a new campaign
Thy guided thunderbolt let fall. O smite
The house and shred it on the smoking plain
That they be all destroyed, forgotten quite
And not one thread of all their thought remain.

Daniel 10-12

saw the Prophet, by the river's strand,
Fallen flat, his strength and senses gone,
By one whose body glowed like a beryl stone
And I heard a voice like waves that beat the sand.
He struggled on hands and knees, then rose to stand;
The angel's eyes were fire and his face shone.
(What help to me these marvellous goings on?
Only the wise, we are told, shall understand.)

Who was the Prince of Persia that could debar
This paragon from passage day by day
When Michael, our Archangel, waited late?
What can I do? I rub my aching scar
Hoping for some protection on the way,
Hoping at last to stand before the gate.

Luke 13:4

It did for them all when it fell down in Siloam.
They were bowling in the still, clear, evening light,
Abner, Balaam, eight Cohens, Jereboam,
Seven of the Levis. I always thought it might.
They tell me God foreknew the stones would tumble.
They say that he did not ordain the day.
It's wind and weather make the limestone crumble
But nobody knows why it suddenly gave way.
They were not sinners more than the rest of the city
The gospels tell us; they're not down in hell.
But four of them owe me money, more's the pity,
Of the friends on whom the tower of Siloam fell.
Was it God's will? was it a worn out wall?
I can only add I always thought it might fall.

Luke 13:6-9

The tree was cursed, the damned thing bore no fruit
Summer to summer, so they've cut it down.
(Last year they watered it and sprayed the crown
And dug in horse manure about the root,
And pruned with care to make the new buds shoot,
And lopped off lower branches bare and brown.)
They are sawing it up to sell the wood in town,
While the gardener scrapes his shovel with his boot.
Now that it's gone, not even the gardener grieves,
Though it went about its work instinctively
And did its duty, or so one believes.
It doubtless tried quite hard like you and me
And had a marvellous great display of leaves
Perhaps more leaves than any other tree.

Acts 12

Up to a point you can't improve the story.
Peter in prison and to die next day:
Calmly between the sleeping guards he lay;
An angel came replete with power and glory
And led him forth to streets with moonlight hoary
Then disappeared. He made his marvellous way
To Rome, that in his name resumed her sway
On all the world, once more her territory.
But furious Herod killed the guardians; eight
As Raphael counted them. Can Athanasius,
Augustine, Ambrose or Tertullian tell
What they had done to suffer such a fate?
Would the great angel not have been more gracious
If he had left one feather in the cell?

Acts 26:7

Instantly serving God in the wilderness,
Intensely burning in the desert night,
Or rising cloudy in the sun's sharp light,
They offered to God their anger and distress.
Erring among the rocks in doubtfulness,
Among their enemies, the Canaanite
Hivite, Jebusite, Amalakite,
Through the uncaring endlessness they press,
Serving God instantly.
                    What then instead?
Would you have had them plan a railway station?
A brewery? a bank? a beach with palms?
And then lie down among the wearied dead?
By this from tribes of slaves stood up a nation;
By this we have the prophets and the psalms.

Acts 26:32

Do not appeal to Caesar, you will lose
Time, money and liberty, perhaps your head;
Appeal to almost anything else instead,
Appeal to abstract justice if you choose,
(Appeal to Sherlock Holmes, give him your clues).
Appeal to the glorious past, the mighty dead,
To unborn generations up ahead,
Or to the Last Great Judgement of the Jews.
But not to Caesar.
                    Paul made that mistake.
Agrippa and Festus would have sent him home
And the great Bernice might have watched and smiled.
But he had appealed to Caesar, he must make
The long rough shipwrecked journey off to Rome.
Do not appeal to Caesar, dearest child!

II Corinthians

Standing in Corinth in the market place
Where the wild blossoms springing fresh and gay
Contend with marble foliage worn away
Which shall exhibit the more ageless grace;
Looking up to the temple's grand worn face
That Paul beheld while preaching day by day;
Seeing the purple waves ride in the bay;
Hearing the light fall of time's lingering pace
Here in the silence,
                    I recall that then
This agora, the ships and crowded strand,
Rang loud with long dispute of weight and price,
The endless energy of commercial men
Whose bales of merchandise from sea and land
Busied their brains. Paul had to write them twice.

Brother Lawrence

He practised the presence of God. I do not know
Whether he moved to the divine mood or whether
God of his grace came where he was. Together
God and the ex-corporal made it so.
Not in some realm of transcendence but here below.
Here at his round of duties his small tight tether
Kept him. Only they sent him in bad weather
To buy wine for the brethren in Bordeaux,
Or was it Belfort?

                Lawrence these centuries dead
Could he return would tell us how it was done,
Give us the formula for bringing power,
Love, joy into the weary head,
Give us the phrase that would call out the sun
And show the eternal springing in the hour.

The Wicket Gate

Good solid Bunyan, but not sound at all
In this. How you reach the road it does not matter.
Bang on the wicket with a cry and a clatter,
Or if they shoot come scrambling over the wall,
Or wander in by a lane. If you have to, crawl
Out of a culvert so flat you can't be flatter,
Your clothes torn on the wire in one vast tatter.
Once on the road you're ready for the long haul.
Then in a sense you can relax, for here,
Strenuous as the going is, you'll end
By safe arrival. Look up, do not fear.
You have a guide, a comrade and a friend.
Though lions roar, though frightful giants appear,
Still waters and green grass are round the bend.

The Road

Sometimes light surprises the child of song,
His notes dissolve in the responding glow.
The heirs of faith, they know the things they know,
The city they go to and where they belong.
My friends will venture north and paddle along
Without a guide, returned, they tell me so.
Miraculous rescues in a ten-foot snow
Are made of the children of fortune, who can't go wrong.

Far otherwise with me. I fall, I stumble;
My best performance plodding toe and heel.
"My extremity God's opportunity," I say.
Yet don't suppose I only mean to grumble;
Often in darkness underfoot I feel
The immemorial stones that pave the Way.

THE MAP NAILED UP

Tapestry

I n Cluny you may see the unicorn
Stand in his tapestry more real than Nature,
The delicate, bold, fiery, fabulous creature,
Unborn, undying, with the spiralled horn.

He is France (and England the gold pard)
He is a royal beast, in him reside
Manifest her gentleness, her pride;
All the great virtues shine in his regard.

And, more than you and I can understand,
Under the pomegranate and the bays
The queen sits while the cold air fills with praise
From the virginals. The horn rests in her hand.

＊

Crossing the quick meridians thread by thread,
I ask what pattern may the poet impose
Upon this north, this land that no one knows,
This land that has no memory of its dead.

We are always in transit as we traffic,
Nothing will stand to talk to or be painted
Except the landscape, aching and unhaunted,
Whose coloured shapes fill out the Geographic.

Speed by enormous boles that pondering stand
Or hold your course high over wintry lakes
Where the white delicate jade still lies in flakes,
Throb with some prow aimed at a stony strand.

     *

What do you see? O I can see the mountains
Delectable, beyond them gates are glowing.
What do you hear? I hear the waters flowing
Where springs the tree of life beside the fountains.

Have you not seen Regina from the air
Spread over acres in a land of snow
While all about the careful angels go
To weave her state below the golden stair?

Have you not seen in old Ontario
The souls of them that from the circling waste
Hewed out that squareness, still with care and haste
About the edges of the storm clouds go?

     *

Not yet the image forms for any eye
Of that mysterious, that heraldic form
Unwoven by the sunlight and the storm.
Renew your journey! Make our shuttle fly!

In August combines weave their gleaming thread
Across the fields; in May the harrows leave
Their dark lines that the mind must interweave.
Clouds file in idle journey overhead.

Clatters the loom as trains to east or west
Trail their long linkage out from side to side;
Down the long lakes, down the St Lawrence' tide,
The wakes of ships weave on and never rest.

*

Weave, weave our flying threads with constant care;
Let the bright shuttle of the aircraft ply
From edge to edge, across our empty sky;
Weave, weave the pattern; there's no time to spare.

And swifter still let your enchanted mind
Fly in the quiet night or active heat,
Before the gathering storm breaks to defeat
Our labour; show the shape yet undefined!

Till like some loved one at an opened door
The royal beast shall stand up from the loom
Magnanimous, dispelling all our gloom,
The unknown one, the one long waited for.

Be Not Disturbed

Be not disturbed, afraid,
Through the desert and bramble ground
Under a hidden moon
Moving without a guide,
For the white dove circling round
In your breast shall settle soon
And the proud lion walk
Gently by your side.

The dove of kindness, flying
Fearlessly through the night
On charmed and tireless wing,
The palm and olive spies
And where cool waters rise,
Gifts hid from day and light,
A hoard to guard from grief
And store on store beyond
In the stony and broken land
Laid there for your relief.

The burning lordly lion
Steps soft on terrible feet.
Not as a tiger springs,
But folding his mighty mane
This comely beast of kings
Wandering beauty wards
Keeps her footsteps safe
From harms, inviolate,
And innocence he guards.

All the journey's length
Go the bird and the royal beast.
Safely you shall rest
Fed by the white dove,
Leaning on the strength
Of the lion, Love.

Ballad of Kingston

Take a morning walk in the elm tree park
Where the lovers have lain in the folded dark;
See the statue standing still and stark.
    Send me better men to work with
    And I will be a better man.

Don't look for an Apollonian grace
Nor yet for Caesar in his face
But read the legend on the base,
    "Send me better men to work with
    And I will be a better man."

As the good historian used to say,
We owe a great deal to old John A.
But he still was made of Canadian clay.
    Send me better men to work with
    And I will be a better man.

Damned compromise in everything,
From Mazarin to Mackenzie King,
And that's why the bells will never ring.
    Send me better men to work with
    And I will be a better man.

In Ottawa, that place of snow,
The palms and the laurels will not grow
And Lampman lies in the grave below.
　　Send me better men to work with
　　And I will be a better man.

If you wait for better men to come
You may wait for a century and then some,
To the end of time and the verge of doom.
　　Send me better men to work with
　　And I will be a better man.

When Christ by the sea of Galilee
Called out to the sons of Zebedee
They were men the same as you and me.
　　(Send me better men to work with
　　And I will be a better man.)

He gave them wine and gave them bread,
He gave them power to raise the dead,
And these are the words he never said:
　　"Send me better men to work with
　　And I will be a better Man."

Isabella Valancy Crawford

ver a store on the corner of King and John
In a couple of rooms upstairs, a trifle shabby,
She was our Brontë, Keats and Chatterton
Without a moor, a nightingale or abbey.
Winds from the lake scoured over frozen ground.
Her mind, within its glass, burned clear and bright
And cast a thrilling brilliance all around
Till Death came up the stairs, put out the light.
Who cared? Who cares? And who can ever care?
Did they? Do you and I? Will anyone?
Light once extinguished dies in deprived air,
The past is self-effacing and soon gone.
Young poet, writing better verse than mine,
Leave for this girl one long resounding line.

For Harold Innis

They say he was a good soldier and a good man,
A good scholar and even a good dean.
I do not know the curve of his high span
Nor over what waters its long flight could lean.
His beginnings and ends and the great all
That lay between elude me. I remember
Only he dragged his lame foot down the hall
To the reading room all through a dark December
In the library. I remember, though long gone,
That he moved across a crowded common room
To ask me, a bird of passage from the West,
How I did. His eyes with simple kindness shone,
With light that quite dissolved the Hart House gloom.
For such things he may be remembered best.

Bird Watching

A thin old bird with a stick and another stick
Flapped feebly over the waves to the insecure
Sloping shelf of our rock. The nest was newer
Than others, drooped down over the menacing slick
Swell of the water. Days passed, a shapeless rick
Of fir twigs, cones, dead grass. The flights grew fewer;
Nest building in depth of December can't endure.
Unseasonable, we said, she's lost the trick.

It may have been so. But on the thirty-first,
Waiting for midnight with a glass in hand,
We suddenly heard the neighbours crying, Fire!
Ran out to see, seaward, the enormous burst
Fling wild and flood with light water and land,
And high in the flame a golden wing shoot higher.

Days Are Simple Cycles

Days are simple cycles of the sun
(Except to newborn infants greeting light);
Every night is just another night
(Except to those who die before it's done);
Each day is other than every other one
(Unless routine has bound the brain up tight);
Night speaks to the heart, its depth or height
(Unless the heart had lost what it had won).
We walk in changing light, no simple bridge
Spanning, touches the far side of fear.
In wind and weather we must hold the ridge
Where walls, on either side, turn, and fall sheer.
Our steps recoil from one, the other edge,
Till oh! the alpine meadows, feeding flocks, appear.

It Is Not Likely

It is not likely you and I will meet,
You are so many and I am so few,
And if we chance to pass upon the street
You would not know me (but I should know you).
I am so few that I am only one,
Though I should like to think that I were more,
Manifold, multiple–but when all's done
A very simple fellow shuts my door
And sits down to assess his own estate,
Cast his accounts, make tea or blow his nose.
Not Alexander, Alfred, Charles the Great,
Only a man still smaller than his clothes.
You are mankind, and each like me his own;
We are one only each in God alone.

Departures Are a Blessing

Departures are a blessing in disguise.
Who leaves now knows he does not leave in vain;
Learning to leave alleviates the pain;
Remaining but defers the enterprise.
Then, having shaken hands and wiped our eyes
And landed otherwhere in pouring rain,
Leaving dear valley for some dreary plain,
At six months' end we move contrariwise
To hills again.
        But when we move above
There shall be no more crossing overseas
And no more sea. Only, impelled by love,
Among those mansions set in healing trees
At will beneath his light we'll stand or move
Whose house is endless and immures all these.

"Dear to God and famous to all ages" – *Milton*

Dear to God and famous to all ages,
Not, alas, an easy integration.
Nice to be recognized across the nation,
Nice to be numbered with the saints and sages,
Nice to be valued for one's marvellous pages,
Nice to possess a golden reputation
Serene and high above the conflagration
And all the civil strife that daily rages.
And dear to God too. That would be the trick.
Dear to the great Creator and Sustainer,
Dear to the source of Light and heart of Love.
Best of both worlds, aware what makes them tick.
But, oh, what expectation could be vainer?
Hold, hold my hand. Then let both worlds remove.

Foxes Have Holes

Foxes have holes, each bird of the air her nest,
Nobody knows where bird or beast has hid
The entrance or the exit. If they did,
Vixens and vireos would never rest.
Man (that's you) has an open box at best
With a roof that taxes or rockets can lift like a lid,
Or expropriation, or the careful quid
Pro quo of the law, for forgery, incest,
Or other cheerful crime.
                            Dreaming of caves
With Monte Cristo, trees with Robin Hood,
Or remote atolls and obedient slaves,
While still I drowse I know I never could
Make or maintain or merit such enclaves.
The path is lost that led deep in the wood.

O Do Not Die

        do not die, for if you did my mirth
Might rise like a river to overflow my land,
From the slant rock sluice off my shallow earth
And leave my acres one long stony strand.
After the funeral I should wonder whose
Funeral we had attended, yours or mine,
And wander vainly picking up the clues
Of the sad irreversible design.
Live for a little, let me hate you less,
And still perhaps a little less, until
Under the slight abrasion without stress
Weakens the steadfast anger of the will
That leaves so little room for you and me
Between the fortress and the ceaseless sea.

"Three lecture hours per week"

Take care when you lift the little copper bottle
You do not wake the genie. He is drowned
In your old drugs and safely under throttle,
Darkened and deadened, all his powers bound.
Pour gently into the teaspoon's silver bowl
And give in lukewarm water thrice a week
The thick dark liquor that might incite the soul
But O take care he does not wake or speak.
Put the top back on quickly. He is a spirit
Able to raise your prostrate crew as kings
And priests that his imperial halls inherit
Filled with unspeakable and glorious things.
Able to wither you with one slight breath.
All they who bound him go down into death.

All Through the 'Thirties

All through the 'thirties, south of Saskatoon,
A farmer farmed a farm without a crop.
Dust filled the air, the lamp was lit at noon,
And never blade of wheat that formed a top.
One New Year's to the hired man he said,
"I have no money. You must take the deeds.
And I will be the hired man instead,
To shovel snow and fork the tumbleweeds."
So it was done. And when the next year came,
"Take back the farm," the other had to say.
And year by year, alternate, just the same
Till the War came and took them both away.
With such superb resource and self-possession
Canada made it through the long depression.

1860's

He stopped on the corner, fearless of detection;
They saw him steadily and saw him whole.
He smiled and acquiesced. The traffic's roll
Was iron hoofs and tires in each direction.
They saw him plain without police protection,
Standing beside an oak tree's ancient bole.
His grey eyes (they would say) were full of soul;
Or (we would say) with interest and affection.
He turned, plunged in the carriages: gone for good.
They too are gone, the Kingsleys, Arnold, all;
Eliot, Collins, Reade. On the small street
Life kindly paused for them and kindly stood,
With his hand on a tree and his back to a brick wall,
Until their time-exposure was complete.

Photographic Exhibition

Please, I implore you! no more nudes on dunes;
And no more smiles where four front teeth are missing
Senile or infantile; no lips for kissing
Painted and poised and posed; no stones with runes;
No brass bands booming out inaudible tunes;
No Pisan fountains innocently pissing,
No study shelves with unread works of Gissing;
No lakes with lengthened shadows and two loons:
I beg of you.
                    But let us have instead
Clear countenances of the human kind
Sculptured by unseen hands through days and seasons
Not only scraped by time. Let the grand head
That home of thought and temple of the Mind
Show life's full moulded form, her incised reasons.

Gift to an Emigrant

Surface crazed with age and counties faded,
He gave his last gift in my ready hand
(And I too young to carry it unaided)
Grandfather's map of England's pleasant land.
Now it is gone but oh! for years hung over
The bed when we came here. I'd lie and trace
From Westmoreland down to the straits of Dover
Line after line the likeness of his face
And think of the grey crag where Michael rested,
Of sanguine dragons on St George's spear,
Then dream of England's clouds with gold invested
Waiting the hour that Christ shall reappear
To sit in glory on his Father's throne
And claim grandfather's England for his own.

Iliad

Go worship Lord Apollo. Let your song
Rise with the incense while the blood runs down.
But pardon me for I must move along
To meet a friend the other side of town.
With wine and something stronger she'll contrive
To calm my nerves and help me to forget
The sight of Marsyas strung up, flayed alive.
(It soaks me every night in a cold sweat.)
Friends of Patroclus too will share our cup
Who knew the towering helmet, the bright spear,
And saw how from behind the god came up –
(The memory dulls, it will not disappear)
How he left greatness naked, ringed with foes.
I go. Look, your Apollo's altar glows!

Advice 1

When you hear knocking on the wall of the cell
Don't think it is only the rain dropping outside
Or the beating of your own heart. Not till you've tried
Listening, digging, and knocking again to tell.
Under the floor with a note like a buoy's far bell
Someone is burrowing. Reach him, you've got a guide,
A wise old friend who'll leave when he has died
The letter, the map, and the means of escape as well.
Dropped for dead, slit sack, with thrust of bursting chest
Reach surface; hail a vessel, gain your isle.
Down in the caves search, search until you find
The treasure—more than any man's possessed—
Move then in Paris with an unseen smile
Till all your foes have died or lost their mind.

 *Advice 2*

ow the old man must die, O do not grieve.
His wisdom slips to sea by the rock's verge,
But spend no time in sorrow. Only believe
That whence he goes he will again emerge
To serve the wronged, the threatened, the confused.
Look onward. There, upon another strand,
The girl revived, the lover yet bemused,
Watch a white sail draw farther from the land.

What the old, wise indomitable man
Gave you, retain and foster till it flower
Deep in your heart; then pass the hard seed on
To germinate in others its pure power.
When the old councillor must veer to sea,
O do not grieve. He goes. And you are he.

Adeste Fideles

In neither joy nor triumph do I come,
Nor yet among the faithful, I'm afraid.
Somehow I must have missed the cavalcade;
The night is dark; I'm a long way from home.
The benefit of clergy, whether Rome,
Byzantium or Canterbury laid
Its hands, has never quite come to my aid.
I grope and stumble in the circling gloom
Circuitous and foiled.
                          Not lost, however!
An intermittent gleam breaks from the hill.
A strong invisible hand lays hold of mine
Even at the instant. My confused endeavour
Moves toward the height where I can see it still,
Sure that its shifting flame will shine for ever.

"Revenge is a kind of wild justice"

ome out! no need for hiding in the bracken.
No one will shoot. Come out and have a chat,
Remembering the words of Francis Bacon,
They'll certainly remind you where you're at.
Come out and bring the dog and bring the cat,
Chop wood in summer, later clear the snow.
I'll lend you axe and shovel, shoes and hat.
(I do not cross you, but I will do so.)

Put on a helmet, let's go down the mine
And see them blast out quartz to get the gold.
Don't be alarmed, the men are friends of mine.
You'll be all right; just do as you are told.
Step in the cage; don't be afraid, be bold,
We only fall ten thousand feet below.
Why do you shake? Is it so very cold?
(I do not cross you, but I will do so.)

Come with me on safari; you shall learn
To shun the mighty rhino running free;
Acquire the art of knowing when to turn
As leopards fall like lightning from the tree,
Or walk between two lions. Come with me
And I will teach you all you ought to know.
At five o'clock we shall be back for tea.
(I do not cross you, but I will do so.)

Do come aboard. The sky is growing clear
And waves I think are somewhat lower now.
The rocks are still invisible. I'll steer
And you can keep a watch up in the bow.
Look out for tow lines looping tug to scow.
And if the engine stalls, well we can row.
You shall be landed safely, that I vow.
(I do not cross you, but I will do so.)

Jump on the chairlift, we will take a trip
Up black Vesuvius and see the cone.
And as we stand right at the crumbling lip,
The steam is rising from the fissures blown.
They say that no eruption ever known
Failed to give warning it was set to go.
Don't worry, you will not be left alone.
(I do not cross you, but I will do so.)

While we are here, beside the flowing Thames,
(A gentle breeze and not a sign of rain)
The flowers about the Tower sway on their stems;
Come see the courtyard famed for Lady Jane.
Why are they carting sawdust? Well, it's plain
They must be putting on some kind of show.
The warder says they've orders to detain . . . ?
Well, do relax. You'll hardly feel the blow.
(I would not cross you, but I must do so.)

Your Map Will Show

Your map will show whatever you want to boast,
Sites of convents,
Seams of coal,
How wholes are divided
Or parts made whole,
Or a northwest passage
An undiscovered goal,
A long, long journey to a far, far coast.
Everyone plots the thing he cares for most.

Your map holds out your absolute hope or fear,
The fall of stocks,
Or rates of divorce,
The track of a meteor
Or a field of force,
The price of freedom
Or the odds on a horse,
Or factors that affect the sale of beer.
Each one charts the thing that he holds dear.

The map nailed up on the wall of the poet's mind
Is a bad prognosis
A fever chart,
Where reels and staggers
An unstable heart
In clear defiance
To the medical art.
Hung upside down and very hard to find,
It records the precise position of all mankind.

Index of titles

Index of titles

87

Index of first lines

Index of first lines

90

These poems are the by-products
of a year of study and travel
made possible by the generosity
of the Canada Council and the
University of British Columbia.

A Note on Publication

This book is the result of a unique association dedicated to
the improvement of the standards of design and manufacture
in the making of Canadian books. It is the third of a group
of selected works of poetry and *belle lettres* chosen both to
inspire and to complement fine craftsmanship in the designing
and manufacturing arts.

It has been published in a limited edition and will not be
reprinted in this format. Its publication is experimental
in the sense that the strict economic limitations that might
normally prevail were waived to permit adequate attention
to detail in the various stages of production.

It was planned and designed by Frank Newfeld, a brilliant
young Canadian designer, typographer and art director,
whose work has earned him an imposing series of awards in
various fields of design.

It was produced under the joint auspices of the Rolland Paper
Company Limited who supplied the stock, Laurentic Japan, Rolland
de Luxe, and Ropaco Offset; T. H. Best Printing Company Limited,
in whose plant the type was set and the books printed and bound;
and McClelland and Stewart Limited.

A Note on the Type

This book is set in Caledonia, a typeface first made
available in 1939. The design is influenced by
Martin's Roman and Scotch Roman and was designed
by the American typographer, W. A. Dwiggins.

The decorative initials, designed by Frank Newfeld
in 1962, are Laurentia.